Table of Contents

FREE GIFT!

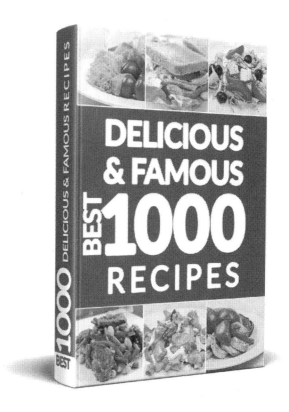

In order to thank you for buying my book I am glad to present you
- BEST Delicious & Famous 1000 Recipes -

Please follow this link to get instant access to your Free Cookbook:
http://booksquare.info/

Introduction

Tapas are traditional and extremely popular bite-sized Spanish hors-d'oeuvres. They are more than just appetizers. When you come to Spain, you will see: tapas are way of eating and a way of living. Nothing could be better having some spicy tapas with a glass of wine in the evening while chatting with your friends.

Tapas are easy to cook using simple ingredients and fun to eat and share.

Tapas are perfect for parties, picnics or an unusual snack within the day. There are no strict rules for making tapas – you can mix chicken, meat, vegetables and fish. Just let your imagination rule!

We made this book for the home use, not restaurants, because tapas are for eating at home with your friends. You will find tapas with eggs for breakfast, tapas with vegetables for light and healthy lunch and, of course, tapas with meat for a tasty dinner!

Have fun!

Octopus "Galician Style"

Healthy, nutritious and delicious! You will definitely enjoy making this traditional tapa originally from the north of Spain

Prep time: 45 minutes
Cooking time: 30 minutes
Servings: 4

Ingredients:
- 1 small octopus (1 Kg.)
- 2 potatoes
- Water
- Salt; salt flakes
- Olive oil
- Sweet paprika powder

Directions:
1. Freeze the octopus the day before preparation time. Unfreeze it 2 hours before preparation.
2. Peel the potatoes and put them in boiling water with salt. Once cooked, cut them into slices
3. Hold the octopus by the head and introduce it on boiling water 3 times until it shrinks.
4. Then, introduce it definitively in boiling water and cook it for 30 minutes.
5. Let it temper down and cut it into pieces with the aid of scissors.
6. To serve, put the potato slices in the base of a wooden dish and place the pieces of octopus on top.
7. Season with a nice stream of olive oil and sprinkle with paprika powder. Season with salt flakes and ... Enjoy!

Nutrition for 100 gr.: Calories: 82, Fat: 1g, Carbohydrates: 2,20g, Protein: 14,91g.

Anchovies in Vinegar

A lovely salty tapa that you would find in almost all tapa - bars in Spain. You can serve them with garlic or with olives, and make happy your friends when they visit you at home!

Prep time: 3 hours
Cooking time: 5 minutes
Servings: 4

Ingredients:
- 1 Kg. of natural anchovies
- Wine vinegar
- Olive oil
- Parsley
- Olives
- Garlic
- Water

Directions:
1. Clean the anchovies with abundant water. Separate the loins and take out the spines. Clean each loin and dry them.
2. Leave them under cold water with ice cubes for 2 hours until they get white.
3. Remove the water and put them in another bowl with 1/3 of water and 2/3 of wine vinegar for about 1 hour.
4. Freeze them in the bowl for 1 day to avoid Anisaki
5. Unfreeze the anchovies
6. Serve with olive oil, garlic and parsley and some olives. Enjoy it!

Nutrition (100 gr.): Calories: 208, Fat: 13,25g, Carbohydrates: 1,56g, Protein: 19,46g.

Clams (sailor style)

Delicious warm tapa that will impress the most exquisite palate. A very special tapa that you will remember forever!

Prep time: 2,5 hours
Cooking time: 15 minutes
Servings: 4

Ingredients:
- 600g. of clams
- ½ onion
- 1 garlic clove
- 1 small chili
- ½ tablespoon of flour
- ½ tablespoon of sweet paprika powder
- 1 tablespoon of tomatoes sauce
- ½ glass of Sherry wine
- Olive oil
- Parsley
- Water
- Bread

Directions:
1. Leave the clams with abundant water for 2 hours. You have to change the water every 30 minutes.
2. Open clams with vapor water and reserve.
3. Slowly fry 1/2 onion, a garlic clove and a small cayenne chili in a pan
4. Add sweet paprika powder and flour until it gets like a paste.
5. Add sherry wine and move until alcohol evaporates.
6. Add tomato sauce, salt and water and leave the mix for 5 minutes.
7. Add the clams for 3-4 minutes more until sauce is consistent... and ready to serve!

8. Serve with 2 slices of bread.

Nutrition (100 gr.): Calories: 92, Fat: 1,20g, Carbohydrates: 3,19g, Protein: 15,83g.

Garlic Prawns

A popular tapa with a delicious sauce for you and your friends to enjoy!
Because tapas is about sharing that fantastic moment!

Prep time: 2 hours
Cooking time: 10 minutes
Servings: 2

Ingredients:
- 400g. of prawns (better fresh than frozen)
- 4 Garlic clove
- 1 small cayenne chili
- ½ glass of white wine
- Olive oil
- Salt
- Bread

Directions:
1. Peel the prawns taking out the heads and reserving the clean body.
2. Clean the prawns with water and leave then for 2 hours in a bowl with water. Then take them out of the water and reserve.
3. In a clay casserole, put the olive oil in a cayenne chili and heat it. Add garlic cloves previously laminated.
4. Once garlic is cooked, add the prawns and heat them up for 3-4 minutes. Add salt and turn up the heat.
5. Turn off the heat. Leave the prawns for about 2 minutes before serving.
6. Add 2 slices of bread and enjoy it!

Nutrition (100 gr.): Calories: 483, Fat: 39,73g, Carbohydrates: 4,47g, Protein: 27,32g.

Spanish Omelet (made with potatoes)

The mother of Spanish tapas! If you learn to cook a great Spanish omelet, you will be welcomed everywhere!

Prep time: 2 hours
Cooking time: 10 minutes
Servings: 4

Ingredients:
- 4 medium size potatoes (700 gr.)
- 2 onions (optional)
- 6 eggs medium size
- Olive oil
- Salt
- Bread

Directions:
1. Peel the onions, slice them and cook them slowly in a big pan with olive oil.
2. Peel the potatoes and slice them. Put the slices in a bowl with water for about 15 minutes.
3. Remove the water from the potatoes and add them to the pan to cook slowly for 15 minutes.
4. Drain potatoes and reserve in a bowl.
5. Beat eggs in a bowl and mix well with onions and potatoes.
6. Put some olive oil in the pan and add the mixture to curdle the omelet for a few minutes.
7. With a plate, turn the omelet to cook the other side.
8. Take out the omelet and cut it into pieces.
9. Serve with some bread.

Nutrition (100 gr.): Calories: 53kcal, Fat: 3,24g, Carbohydrates: 6,14g, Protein: 1,33g.

Croquettes of Ham

The most famous Spanish tapa! If you learn to cook a great Spanish Omelet, you will be welcome everywhere!

Prep time: 2 hours
Cooking time: 10 minutes
Servings: 4

Ingredients:
- 200 g of Serrano ham
- 1 onion
- 3 eggs
- Olive oil
- Salt
- Bread
- 1 garlic clove
- 100 gr. flour
- 100 g butter
- 1 l of milk
- Olive Oil

Directions:
1. Cut the butter into cubes and put it to melt in a pan.
2. Chop the onion and garlic clove. Fry for 5-6 minutes, and add Serrano ham.
3. Add flour and stir well. Add slowly milk and keep stirring. Keep adding milk and stirring until you get bechamel. Cook for 20 minutes.
4. Spread the dough onto a flat container and let it cool.
5. When the dough is cold, cut and mold the croquettes.
6. Moist the dough into egg and breadcrumbs and fry them in abundant hot oil.
7. Once they are done, remove them from the frying pan and put them on a plate with kitchen paper to remove excess oil. Enjoy it!

Nutrition (100 gr.): Calories: 240 kcal, Fat: 13,90g, Carbohydrates: 21,60g, Protein: 6,80g.

Aioli Potatoes

A quick and classic Mediterranean tapa. The secret is in a perfect cooking of the potatoes. Do you dare with the challenge?

Prep time: 10 minutes
Cooking time: 1 hour
Servings: 4

Ingredients:
- 4 medium size potatoes (700 gr.)
- Fresh parsley
- Salt
- 1 egg
- 150 ml. sunflower oil
- 1 lemon

Directions:
1. Cook the potatoes in a pot with plenty of water and 1 tablespoon of salt for 20-30 minutes.
2. Remove the water and let them cool
3. Peel the potatoes by pulling the skin with a small knife. Reserve.
4. To prepare the aioli, put the egg, the clove of garlic and the 150 ml of sunflower oil in the glass of the mixer. Add a few drops of lemon juice and salt
5. Beat at medium speed, having the mixer straight. Do not move it.
6. Once it is mixed, move the mixer slowly from bottom to top to incorporate the oil from the surface.
7. Serve in a bowl, mixing the potatoes with 3 or 4 tablespoons of aioli and chopped parsley. Store in the fridge for 1 hour before consumption

Nutrition (100 gr.): Calories: 716kcal, Fat: 78,00g, Carbohydrates: 15,61g, Protein: 2,33g.

Seafood Paella

Paella is known throughout the world for its taste! Healthy and authentic, the best you can cook to your partner!

Prep time: 30 minutes
Cooking time: 1,5 hours
Servings: 4

Ingredients:
- 400 gr. rice
- 2 garlic cloves
- 2-3 tomatoes
- 1 red pepper
- 500 gr. squid
- 8 prawns
- 16 clams
- 1,5 l. fish soup
- Saffron
- ½ tablespoon sweet paprika
- 1 pinch of food coloring
- Olive oil
- Salt

Directions:
1. For preparation, clean all the seafood. Chop tomatoes, pepper and garlic.
2. Fry prawns and in a pan with olive oil a couple of minutes on each side. Reserve.
3. Add pepper and stir-fry during few minutes. Add garlic, stir-fry for 1 minute, and add tomatoes and sweet paprika. Cook the mix for 5 minutes.
4. Add the clams and the squid and stir-fry.
5. Add the rice to the mix and stir-fry the rice.
6. Add fish soup and distribute the mixture well throughout the pan.

7. Add salt to taste and food coloring. Put the high heat until it begins to boil.
8. Then cook slowly for 15 minutes. Please do not stir the mix any longer. Add prawns to the top, and let it cook for 5 more minutes.
9. Once finished, cover with a clean kitchen towel and let stand 5 minutes before serving.

Nutrition (250 gr.): Calories: 366kcal, Fat: 14,00g, Carbohydrates: 48,50g, Protein: 8,80g.

Black Rice

In spite of its appearance, this delicious dish will conquer your palate.
Healthy, nutritious and simply unique!

Prep time: 30 minutes
Cooking time: 1,5 hours
Servings: 4

Ingredients:
- 400 gr. rice
- 2 garlic cloves
- 2-3 tomatoes
- 1 onion
- 500 gr. cuttlefish
- 4 squid ink sachets
- 1,5 l. fish soup
- Saffron
- Olive oil
- Salt

Directions:
1. Clean the cuttlefish under the running tap water, dry very well and cut into small pieces. Put it in a big pan with olive oil and cook slowly.
2. Peel onion and garlic. Chop the onion thinly and cut the garlic into slices. Add them to the pan.
3. Add chopped tomatoes and mix for 2 or 3 minutes.
4. Add the rice to the mix and stir-fry the rice.
5. Add fish soup and squid ink and distribute the mixture well throughout the pan.
6. Add salt to taste and saffron. Put the high heat until it begins to boil.
7. Then cook slowly for 20 minutes. Please do not stir the mix any longer.

8. Once finished, cover with a clean kitchen towel and let stand 5 minutes before serving.
9. Serve with aioli.

Nutrition (250 gr.): Calories: 299kcal, Fat: 10,00g, Carbohydrates: 41,00g, Protein: 10,50g.

Tuna Fish with Tomato

Tuna fish with tomato, one of the classics of the grandmothers, one of the homemade recipes that have been made in my house of a lifetime and that I love

Prep time: 15 minutes
Cooking time: 30 minutes
Servings: 2

Ingredients:
- 700 gr. Tuna fish
- 1 onion
- 2 garlic cloves
- 500 gr. fried tomato (canned)
- Olive oil
- Salt
- Flour
- Bread

Directions:
1. In a frying pan put garlic, cloves (do not peel them). Once golden, retire.
2. Put salt and flour in the pieces of tuna and introduce them in the hot pan to seal. Once sealed, reserve.
3. In a saucepan, cook slowly previously laminated onion, until it is transparent.
4. Add fried tomato to the onion and cook it for 2-3 minutes.
5. Add tuna fish to the saucepan and cook them for 2-3 minutes.
6. Serve with bread and enjoy it!

Nutrition (500 gr.): Calories: 772kcal, Fat: 36,80g, Carbohydrates: 51,90g, Protein: 52,80g.

Artichokes with Ham

Artichokes with ham and onion is a classic recipe. The salty Serrano ham makes the flavor of the artichoke be enhanced, so it is perfect!

Prep time: 15 minutes
Cooking time: 15 minutes
Servings: 2

Ingredients:
- 12 fresh artichokes.
- 100 gr. of Serrano ham on tacos.
- 1 onion.
- 2 garlic cloves.
- 1-tablespoon lemon juice.
- Olive oil
- Salt
- Freshly ground black pepper.

Directions:
1. Clean the artichokes with your own hands. Put them in a bowl filled with water with the lemon juice, to prevent them from rusting.
2. In a pot, put plenty of water with high heat until boil, split the artichokes in half and place them in the pot. Let it cook for about 15 minutes.
3. Peel the onion and the garlic and cut into slices. Fry them in a pan with olive oil.
4. Add Serrano ham and let it cook all together for 2-3 minutes. Reserve.
5. Remove water from artichokes and add them to the pan.
6. Add salt and pepper to taste. Stir. Are you ready? Enjoy it!

Nutrition (100 gr.): Calories: 153kcal, Fat: 14,00g, Carbohydrates: 3,90g, Protein: 1,70g.

Crispy Goat Cheese with Caramelized Onion

Impossible to resist the crisp bite of this skewer and then enjoy the creaminess of the melted cheese! An exquisite appetizer! Easy to prepare and to eat.

Prep time: 5 minutes
Cooking time: 15 minutes
Servings: 2

Ingredients:
- 1 roll of goat's cheese
- Egg and bread crumbs
- Garlic and Parsley (optional)
- ½ onion
- Brown sugar (or white)
- Balsamic vinegar

Directions:
1. Cut the onion into very thin sheets. Pour the onion with a little oil, and when it is transparent add the sugar. Remove and let caramelize. Add a trickle of Modena vinegar and let thicken. Reserve.
2. We cut the goat cheese curl into portions of a centimeter.
3. Pass cheese disks for egg and breadcrumbs. Use breadcrumbs of garlic and parsley to add flavor to the cheese.
4. Freeze cheese disk for about 10 minutes before frying them. In this way, they will not be broken while we fry them.
5. Fry in abundant oil one minute by each side. Take them out to a plate covered with absorbent paper to remove the excess oil.
6. Serve with the caramelized onion on top.

Nutrition (100 gr.): Calories: 309kcal, Fat: 25,00g, Carbohydrates: 1,00g, Protein: 20,00g.

Crunchy Prawns

The secret lies in the accompanying sauces!

Prep time: 15 minutes
Cooking time: 15 minutes
Servings: 4

Ingredients:
- 300 gr. cooked prawns
- Brick pastry or wafers for dumplings
- 1 egg
- 2 garlic cloves
- Olive oil
- Sauces: Soy sauce, spicy chili and curry-mango.

Directions:
1. Peel all the prawns leaving the end of the tail to be able to pick up later.
2. Separate the dough and beat the egg with the help of a fork
3. Peel and chop the garlic cloves in two. Rub them in the dough and then spread a little-beaten egg.
4. Roll each of the prawns with the dough. Pass them by beaten egg to seal well and let them drain well before putting them in the pan.
5. Fry the prawns over high heat in abundant olive oil. Remove them from the oil with a kitchen paper.
6. Serve with nice sauces: soy sauce, spicy chili and curry-mango.

Nutrition (100 gr.): Calories: 225kcal, Fat: 8,21gr. Carbohydrates: 25,48g, Protein: 11,22g.

Tumaca Bread

Tumaca Bread is one of the most popular breakfasts you can find in Catalonia. Easy to make and tasty. You'll love it!

Prep time: 5 minutes
Cooking time: 10 minutes
Servings: 2

Ingredients:
- 2-3 Tomatoes
- Garlic
- Olive oil
- Serrano ham
- 4 slices of bread

Directions:
1. Mash the peeled tomato with the garlic and the olive oil.
2. Toast the 4 pieces of bread.
3. Spread on the toast the mixture we have made with the tomatoes.
4. Add Serrano ham on top and enjoy it!

Nutrition (100 gr.): Calories: 123kcal, Fat: 2,66gr. Carbohydrates: 13,56g, Protein: 12,98g.

Andalusian Gazpacho

Everything you need when summer starts. Easy, fast, uncomplicated and very refreshing. The original Andalusian gazpacho is perfect to drink at any time of the day!

Prep time: 5 minutes
Cooking time: 10 minutes
Servings: two

Ingredients:
- 50 gr. soft crust bread
- 1 kg. pear tomatoes
- 35 - 50 ml Sherry vinegar
- 1/2 teaspoon Salt.
- 1 Garlic clove
- 50 gr. onion
- 50 gr. Green pepper
- 100 gr Cucumber
- 100 ml olive oil
- Very cold water, optional

Directions:
1. Wash the vegetables well, peel and cut them into pieces.
2. Put bread and peeled tomatoes in the bowl of a blender and grind.
3. Add Sherry vinegar, salt, the clove of garlic, the onion, the green pepper and the cucumber. Grind until cream has a homogeneous texture.
4. To finish, integrate the olive oil that we will add gradually while we continue beating.
5. Leave it in the refrigerator until the moment of serving, because the colder, richer it will be.
6. Serve with a few small pieces of tomato, cucumber and onion

Nutrition (250 gr.): Calories: 110kcal, Fat: 6,00gr. Carbohydrates: 9,60g, Protein: 2,80g.

Garlic Mushrooms

A super simple recipe that can serve as a side dish of meat or poultry, or accompanied by pasta, white rice or mashed potatoes!

Prep time: 5 minutes
Cooking time: 10 minutes
Servings: 2

Ingredients:
- 300 gr mushrooms
- 5 garlic cloves
- 1/3 cup olive oil
- Salt
- Black pepper
- Fresh parsley
- Parmesan (optional)

Directions:
1. Clean the mushrooms remove the stem and cut them into 4 pieces.
2. Peel and laminate the garlic. Put the laminated garlic in a pan with hot oil for 1 minute
3. Add mushrooms, salt, black pepper and the parsley. Let it cook for 5 minutes.
4. Serve with a bit of parmesan on top.

Nutrition (100 gr.): Calories: 22kcal, Fat: 0,34gr. Carbohydrates: 3,28g, Protein: 3,09g.

Spicy Sardines with Tomatoes

A super simple recipe that can serve as a side dish of meat or poultry, or accompanied by pasta, white rice or mashed potatoes!

Prep time: 15 minutes
Cooking time: 45 minutes
Servings: 4

Ingredients:
- 1 Kg. Fresh clean sardines - without guts and without head
- 800 gr. Tomatoes crushed without skins or seeds
- 100 ml olive oil
- 3 Garlic cloves
- 2-3 Chilies
- Salt to taste
- 1/2 teaspoon sugar
- Bread

Directions:
1. In a large casserole heat olive oil with the garlic cut into a couple of pieces and the chilies. Cook for 1 minute.
2. Add crushed tomatoes. Stir- fry the tomato for about 30 minutes over medium-low heat
3. Lightly salt the sardines and add them to tomato sauce. Cook them for few minutes and turn off the heat. Leave them 2 more minutes.
4. Let them cool down and put them in the fridge
5. Serve with a slice of toasted bread

Nutrition (100 gr.): Calories: 178kcal, Fat: 10,00gr. Carbohydrates: 0,90g, Protein: 21,00g.

Stuffed Eggs

Easy and fast, you will triumph!

Prep time: 10 minutes
Cooking time: 20 minutes
Servings: 2

Ingredients:
- 6 large eggs
- 200 gr. of tuna in olive oil
- 1 canned red pepper
- Salt to taste
- Mayonnaise

Directions:
1. Cook the eggs and peel them once they are cold
2. Open them in half and we take out all the yolks with care of not breaking the whites
3. In a separate bowl, we put the yolks, reserving one, the very well drained tuna, chopped red pepper, three tablespoons of mayonnaise and a pinch of salt.
4. Mix everything very well with the help of a fork. Press the ingredients to undo.
5. Fill each egg half with this mixture.
6. Cover with a little mayonnaise and garnish with strips of pepper and grated yolk.
7. Keep them in the refrigerator until the right moment to serve.

Nutrition: Calories: 62kcal, Fat: 5,03gr. Carbohydrates: 0,42g, Protein: 3,59g.